PLAYS FOR PERFORMANCE

*A series designed for
contemporary production and study
Edited by
Nicholas Rudall and Bernard Sahlins*

AUGUST STRINDBERG

Miss Julie

In a New Translation by
Truda Stockenström

Ivan R. Dee
CHICAGO

Library of Congress Cataloging-in-Publication Data:
Strindberg, August, 1849–1912.
    [Fröken Julie. English]
    Miss Julie / August Strindberg : in a new translation by Truda Stockenström.
        p. cm. — (Plays for performance)
        ISBN 1-56663-110-6 (alk. paper). — ISBN 1-56663-109-2 (pbk. : alk. paper)
    I. Stockenström, Truda. II. Title. III. Series.
PT9812.F8E5 1996
839.72´6—dc20   95-49227

INTRODUCTION
by Truda Stockenström and Goran Stockenström

"Because they are modern characters living in a period of transition more feverishly hysterical . . . I have drawn my figures vacillating, disintegrated, a blend of old and new. My souls (characters) are conglomerations of past and present stages of civilization, bits from books and newspapers, scraps of humanity, rags and tatters of fine clothing, patched together as is the human soul."

—August Strindberg

Miss Julie (1888), written more than a hundred years ago, presents the tragic affair of a young countess and her servant in a Swedish manor house on Midsummer Eve. August Strindberg, its young radical author, was then thirty-nine and living in exile in Germany. His own marriage to Siri Von Essen, an actress, from a noble family, was on the verge of a breakdown. The psychological and social conflicts of the play draw upon strands of Strindberg's own life and examine his feelings into the very heart of darkness and beyond.

This concentrated play is so universal that it may be staged in different settings. It is one climactic scene, with pantomime, dance, and monologues offering the only relief in a psychological crescendo where the sex act serves as a peripety and suicide as a catharsis. An uninterrupted flow of action takes us through the different phases of sexual relationships as we recog-

3

nize them from myth, history, and our own lives. The first stage consists of romance with exquisite role-playing, mirroring, and the projection of images in a web of unspoken fantasies and assumptions. The next stage reveals the hidden power struggle when love turns to hate and illusions are replaced by humiliations and punishments in a sadomasochistic *danse macabre.* The powers of darkness engulf the protagonists in their desperate struggle to find an answer to the question about God and Man that has been formulated in a long succession of tragedies before them. For Strindberg, the protagonists are only individuals in a world devoid of God, if not guilt.

Jean and Julie are modern characters living in a period of transition and social upheaval in which the shaping forces of our own culture can easily be perceived. Politically the old elite had lost some of its power in Sweden through the parliamentary reorganization of 1866. Emerging was a new ruling class represented by workers. The emancipation movement sought political redress and urged a new role for women. Clinging to values of the old order, Jean and Julie are tragically doomed.

Strindberg's preface to *Miss Julie* was written after the fact and was in many ways a political manifesto. It attempted to place *Miss Julie* in the avant-garde of naturalism and promote it to the Theater Libre. Strindberg succeeded in both these respects but did it so admirably that the play has been reduced in history to a school example of naturalism, or no more than a play about the conflict between social classes with its character reduced to neurotic case studies.

In the quote above from Strindberg's preface, he seems to contend that man is a continent integrating the psychological, ideological, social, and political worlds within his consciousness at an intersection of historical change. Jean's and Julie's life stories reflect this situation but offer little solace and no explanation for the tragedy. The logic of cause and effect serves well on the level of plot, but when even language fails to communicate, a future is not to be found in structures from natural science but in such outmoded aesthetics as myth and religion.

Not even the stage setting attempts an objective representation of an identifiable reality, otherwise the easiest part of the naturalistic dogma to realize. Instead Strindberg chooses asymmetric lines from impressionist painting—a corner of nature without beginning or end. As a painter Strindberg knew that reality tended to break down into fleeting impressions on the retina of the eye, and that at times it was impossible to differentiate between sensation and illusion. By selecting symbolic properties to materialize the entrapped souls, Strindberg intensifies *the real* as an impressionist painting might—not an imitation of reality but a vision of reality.

The many scientific explanations for Julie's tragic end may serve only as intellectual discourse. In retrospect they may be analogous to Julie's monologue *in presto tempo* to convince herself there is an alternative to suicide. On the stage they are of no use. At the final moment Julie is utterly alone in a state of trance, holding the razor to cut her throat while Jean remains equally alone in frozen terror before a bell: "To be so frightened of a bell! Yes, but it's not just a bell. There's somebody behind it. A hand sets it in motion. And something else sets the hand in motion. Cover your ears—cover your ears! But he'll just ring louder! . . ." The bell represents the Count, the absent but ever-present idea that offers no explanation but points to another system unknown to the participants in the final deadly ritual. A world disintegrates and human life returns to earth, but beyond glimmers of a spiritual truth. At that moment on stage it is only through the collective experience of the actors and the craft of the theatre that the tragedy of *Miss Julie* achieves that power beyond words that we can experience in our hearts and souls but never rationally explain.

Miss Julie is a rich living classic whose sequels in modern drama include Sartre's *No Exit* (1944), Genet's *The Maids* (1947), and Tennessee Williams's *A Streetcar Named Desire* (1947). It presents a challenge for any ensemble to search for the roots in their art in a time when so many theatres have forgotten that their art is not that of the impossible, as many postmodernists would have us believe. O'Neill's motto for his last cycle of plays on the American experience, "A Tale of Possessors Self-Dispossessed," raises the same biblical question as Strindberg's *Miss Julie*: "What does it matter if man gains the world and loses his soul."

My intent in this translation is to be faithful to the original text while retaining its rhythm and emotional feeling. The language is sometimes quite real, sometimes heightened, yet always immediate. The text is also aggressive and explosive. Strindberg speaks in contrasting tones, and at times the lines are filled with abrupt style shifts that reflect the fragmentation and play-acting of the characters. Their social and psychological backgrounds emerge through their choice of words. When Jean speaks to Julie early in the play, he speaks in an entirely different way than with Kristine. The image of the language is very similar to that of an impressionist painting but has the feel of a piece of music. It is a contemporary translation for actors, created through two different productions of the play.

CHARACTERS

MISS JULIE, *age twenty-five*
JEAN, *the valet, age thirty*
KRISTINE, *the cook, age thirty-five*

This translation of *Miss Julie* was produced by the Court Theatre, Chicago, with the help of Kate Collins, Tanya White, Johnny Lee Davenport, Carmen Roman, and Charlie Newell. The Geddes Agency, Debbie Proudian, Kerstin Lane, Kurt Mathiasson, and the Swedish American Museum Center helped with the original production of this translation by the Intimate Theater. Thanks too to Ruth Jacobson, John Kavanagh, and most of all to my father Goran Stockenström for his love, passion, and knowledge of Strindberg and for his support and inspiration.

Miss Julie

The large kitchen of a Swedish manor house in a country district in the late 1880s. Midsummer Eve.

The kitchen has three doors, two small ones into Jean's and Kristine's bedroom, and a large glass-fronted double one, opening onto a courtyard. This is the only way to the rest of the house. Through these glass doors can be seen part of a fountain with a cupid, lilac bushes in flower, and the tops of some Lombardy poplars. On one wall are shelves edged with scalloped paper on which are kitchen utensils of copper, iron, and tin. To the left is the corner of a large tiled range and part of its chimney hood; to the right is the servants' dinner table with chairs beside it. The stove is decorated with birch boughs, the floor strewn with twigs of juniper. On the end of the table is a large Japanese spice jar full of lilac. There are also an icebox, a scullery table, and a sink. Above the double door hangs a big old-fashioned bell; near it is a speaking tube.

A fiddle can be heard from the dance in the barn nearby.

Kristine is standing at the stove, frying something in a pan. She wears a light-colored cotton dress and a big apron.

Jean enters, wearing a uniform and carrying a pair of large riding boots with spurs, which he puts in a conspicuous place.

JEAN: Miss Julie's running wild again. She's gone crazy!

KRISTINE: Oh, so you finally came back?

JEAN: I took the Count to the station and on my way back I stopped at the barn for a dance. Who do I see but Miss Julie leading off the dance with the gamekeeper! As soon as she sets eyes on me she rushes over and asks to dance the Lady's Waltz with me. And how she waltzed! I've never seen anything like it. She's crazy.

KRISTINE: That's nothing new, but she's been worse than ever since her engagement was broken off two weeks ago.

JEAN: Yes, there's a story to be told! He was a gentleman, even if he wasn't rich. Ah! They have such peculiar ideas. *(Jean sits on the table)* Still, it's strange that on Midsummer Eve she's staying home with the servants instead of going with her father to visit her relatives.

KRISTINE: She's probably embarrassed after that fiasco with her fiancé.

JEAN: Probably! He gave a good account of himself, though. Do you know what happened, Kristine? I saw the whole thing, though I didn't let on.

KRISTINE: No! You saw it?

JEAN: You bet I did. I came across the pair of them one evening in the stableyard. Miss Julie was "training" him—that's what she called it. Do you know what that was? Making him jump over her riding crop—the way you'd teach a dog. He jumped twice and each time she hit him. But the third time he leapt up, grabbed the crop out of her hand, hit her with it across the cheek, and broke it to pieces. Then he left.

KRISTINE: So that's how it happened! Well, what do you know!

JEAN: Yes, that was the end of that. *(pause)* Now, what have you got for me, Kristine? Something tasty?

12

KRISTINE: *(serving him from the pan)* Oh, it's just a piece of kidney I cut off their veal roast.

JEAN: *(smelling the food)* Wonderful! That's my favorite *delice. (feeling the plate)* But you might have warmed the plate!

KRISTINE: When you're in the mood you can be more finicky than the Count. *(she pulls his hair affectionately)*

JEAN: *(angry)* Stop it, leave my hair alone! You know how sensitive I am.

KRISTINE: Now, now. It's just because I love you.

(Jean eats; Kristine opens a bottle of beer)

JEAN: Beer? On Midsummer Eve? No thank you! I can do better than that. *(opens a drawer and takes out a bottle of red wine with yellow sealing wax)* See that? Gold seal! Now get me a glass. *(she hands him a tumbler)* No, a wine glass, of course!

KRISTINE: *(returns to the stove and puts on a small saucepan)* God help the woman that gets you for a husband! You're so fussy!

JEAN: Nonsense! You'd be damned lucky to get a man like me. Anyhow, it hasn't hurt you—telling people we're engaged. *(tastes wine)* Good! Very good! But not quite the right temperature. *(warms it with his hands)* We bought this in Dijon. Four francs a liter, not counting the cost of the bottle or the customs duty. What are you cooking now? It stinks like hell!

KRISTINE: Oh, some damnable crap Miss Julie wants for her dog Diana.

JEAN: You should watch your language, Kristine. But why do you have to cook for that damn bitch dog on Midsummer Eve? Is it sick?

KRISTINE: Yes, it's sick! She sneaked out with the game-keeper's mutt and got knocked up. Miss Julie just won't have it!

JEAN: Miss Julie has too much pride about some things, and not enough about others. Just like her mother. The Countess was more at home in the kitchen and at the cowsheds than anywhere else. But a one-horse carriage wasn't elegant enough for her. Her cuffs were always dirty, but she had to have the coat of arms on her cufflinks. And Miss Julie, to get back to her, doesn't have any respect for herself or her position either. If you ask me, she just isn't refined. In the barn just now she pulled Anna away from the gamekeeper and made him dance with her. We wouldn't behave like that, but that's what happens when aristocrats pretend they're common people—they get *common*! Still, she's quite a woman! Statuesque! What shoulders, and what . . . etcetera!

KRISTINE: Oh, don't overdo it! I've heard what Clara says, and she dresses her.

JEAN: Clara? Ha! You're all just jealous of her! I've been out riding with her . . . and the way she dances!

KRISTINE: Listen, Jean! You're going to dance with me when I'm finished here, aren't you?

JEAN: Of course.

KRISTINE: Promise?

JEAN: Promise? When I say I'm going to do something, I do it! By the way, the kidney was very good. *(he corks the bottle)*

(Miss Julie appears at the doorway, speaks offstage)

14

JULIE: I'll be right back! Don't wait for me. *(Jean sneaks the bottle back into the table drawer and gets up respectfully. Miss Julie enters and crosses to Kristine by the stove.)* Well, is it ready? *(Kristine indicates that Jean is present)*

JEAN: *(gallantly)* Are you ladies up to something secret?

JULIE: *(flipping his face with her handkerchief)* None of your business!

JEAN: Hmmm! I like the smell of violets!

JULIE: *(flirting)* Shame on you! So you're an expert on perfumery as well? You certainly know how to dance. Ah, ah! No peeking! Go away.

(sound of a schottische begins in the distance)

JEAN: *(cocky but respectful)* Are you ladies cooking up a witches' brew for Midsummer Eve? Something to prophesy by under a lucky star, so you'll catch a glimpse of your future husband!

JULIE: *(sharply)* You'd need good eyes to see that! *(to Kristine)* Pour out half a bottle and cork it tight. *(to Jean)* Jean, come and dance a schottische with me.

JEAN: *(hesitates)* I hope you don't think me rude, but I've promised this dance to Kristine. . . .

JULIE: Well, she can always get somebody else. Isn't that right, Kristine? You'll lend me Jean, won't you?

KRISTINE: It's not up to me, ma'am. *(to Jean)* If the mistress is gracious enough to invite you, it wouldn't do for you to say no. You go on, and thank her for the honor.

JEAN: To be honest—and no offense intended—I wonder whether it's wise for you to dance twice in a row with the same partner. Especially since the people around here are so quick to jump to conclusions. . . .

JULIE: *(flaring up)* What's that? What sort of conclusions? What do you mean?

JEAN: *(submissively)* Since my lady chooses not to understand, I'll have to speak more plainly. Since all your servants are hoping for the same honor, it doesn't look good for you to play favorites with one of them.

JULIE: Play favorites! What an idea! I'm astonished! As mistress of the house, I honor your dance with my presence. And if I feel like dancing, I want to dance with someone who knows how to lead, so I won't look ridiculous.

JEAN: As my lady orders. I'm at your service!

JULIE: *(gently)* Don't take it as an order! Tonight we're all just happy people celebrating. So let's forget about rank. Now, give me your arm!—Don't worry, Kristine! I won't run off with your boyfriend!

(Jean gives Julie his arm. They exit.)

(Left alone, Kristine goes about her work, occasionally humming along with the distant music that is mixed with low laughter and sometimes a distant shout. She clears Jean's place and washes the dishes and puts them away. She takes off her apron. From the top drawer she gets a small mirror and a comb. She props the mirror against the vase of lilacs in the center of the table. Sitting down, she dresses her hair, using the mirror. She lights a candle and heats a hairpin, with which she curls her bangs. She walks to the door where she looks out and listens. After a while she returns to the table. She finds the handkerchief Julie left behind, picks it up and smells it. Then, preoccu-

16

pied, she spreads it out automatically, stretches it, smoothes out the wrinkles, and folds it into quarters. Meanwhile the music has stopped. A few minutes of distant voices and night sounds, and Jean enters.)

JEAN: God, she really *is* crazy! What a way to dance! Everybody's laughing at her behind her back. What do you make of it, Kristine?

KRISTINE: Oh, it's that time of the month for her. She always gets peculiar like that. Are you going to dance with me now?

JEAN: You're not mad at me for leaving, are you . . . ?

KRISTINE: Of course not! Why should I be, for a little thing like that? Besides, I know my place.

JEAN: *(grabs her around her waist from behind)* Oh you're a sensible girl, Kristine. You'll make a good wife.

(Miss Julie enters, unpleasantly surprised, with forced good humor)

JULIE: What a charming escort—running away from your partner.

JEAN: On the contrary, Miss Julie. As you can see, I've hurried back to the partner I deserted.

JULIE: *(changing her tone)* You know, no one else dances like you do! But why are you wearing your uniform on a holiday? Take it off at once!

JEAN: Then I must ask you to leave for a moment. My black coat is hanging over here. . . . *(gestures and crosses right)*

JULIE: Are you embarrassed about changing your coat in front of me? Well, go into your room then. Or else stay here and I'll turn my back.

17

JEAN: With your permission, ma'am! *(He crosses right. His arm is visible as he changes his jacket.)*

JULIE: Tell me, Kristine. Jean acts so familiar with you. Are the two of you engaged?

KRISTINE: Engaged? If you like. We call it that.

JULIE: What do you mean?

KRISTINE: Well, you've been engaged yourself, Miss Julie. . . .

JULIE: But we were *properly* engaged. . . .

KRISTINE: Yes. Didn't come to anything, though, did it?

(enter Jean, dressed in a frock coat and bowler hat)

JULIE: *Tres gentil, Monsieur Jean. Tres gentil.*

JEAN: *Vous voulez plaisanter, Madam.*

JULIE: *Et vous voulez parler français.* Where did you learn that?

JEAN: In Switzerland. I was sommelier in one of the biggest hotels in Lucerne!

JULIE: You look quite the gentleman in that outfit! *Charmant! (she sits at the table)*

JEAN: Oh, you're just flattering me!

JULIE: *(slightly annoyed)* Flattering you?

JEAN: My natural modesty forbids me to presume you would actually compliment someone like me, so I took the liberty of assuming you were exaggerating, for which I believe the polite word is "flattery."

JULIE: *(with a light laugh)* Where did you learn to talk like that? You must have seen a lot of plays.

18

JEAN: Yes, indeed! And I've visited many places as well.

JULIE: But you were born in this area, weren't you?

JEAN: My father was a farmhand on the district attorney's estate next door to yours. Of course you didn't notice me, but I used to see you when you were little.

JULIE: No! Really?

JEAN: Yes. I remember one time in particular—but I can't tell you about that.

JULIE: Oh, come on! Of course you can. Just this once!

JEAN: No, I really couldn't, not now. Some other time, perhaps.

JULIE: Another time means never. What's the harm in now?

JEAN: There's no harm, but there are obstacles. Look at that! *(points at Kristine, who has fallen asleep in a chair by the stove)*

JULIE: She'll make a pleasant wife, won't she? She probably snores too.

JEAN: No, she doesn't. But she talks in her sleep.

JULIE: *(cynically)* How would *you* know she talks in her sleep?

JEAN: *(coolly)* I've heard her! $\leftarrow$ S / T

JULIE: *(after a pause)* Why don't you sit down?

JEAN: I wouldn't take that liberty in your presence.

JULIE: Not even if I ordered you?

JEAN: Then I'd obey.

19

JULIE: Sit down, then.—No, wait. Can you get me something to drink first?

JEAN: I don't know what we have in the icebox. Only beer, I think.

JULIE: There's no "only" about it. I have very simple tastes. I prefer it to wine.

(Jean takes a bottle of beer from the icebox and opens it. He looks for a glass and a plate in the cupboard and serves her.)

JEAN: At your service.

JULIE: Thank you. Won't you have some yourself?

JEAN: I'm not partial to beer, but if it's an order . . .

JULIE: An order? Surely you know that a gentleman should never allow a lady to drink alone.

JEAN: A point well taken. *(opens a bottle and gets a glass)*

JULIE: Now drink to my health! *(he hesitates)* What? A man of the world—and shy?

(in mock romantic fashion, he kneels and raises his glass)

JEAN: To my lady's health! *(he drinks)*

JULIE: Bravo! Now kiss my shoe and everything will be perfect. *(Jean hesitates, then boldly seizes her foot and kisses it lightly)* Excellent! You should have been an actor.

JEAN: *(rising)* This has got to stop, Miss Julie! Someone might come in and see us.

JULIE: So what?

JEAN: People would talk, that's what! If you only knew how their tongues were wagging out there just a few minutes ago.

JULIE: What were they saying? Tell me!—Sit down!

JEAN: *(sitting)* I don't want to hurt your feelings, but they were saying things—suggestive things, that ... well, you can figure it out for yourself! You're not a child. If a woman is seen drinking alone with a man—and a servant at that—in the middle of the night . . . well . . .

JULIE: Well what? Besides, we're not alone. Kristine is here.

JEAN: Asleep!

JULIE: I'll wake her up. *(rises to Kristine)* Kristine! Are you asleep?

(Kristine mumbles sleepily)

JULIE: Kristine!—She certainly can sleep!

KRISTINE: *(as if in sleep)* The Count's boots are cleaned —put the coffee on—quick, quick, quick. . . . *(laughs, then grunts)* . . . mm-mm. Poofff . . .

JULIE: *(grabbing Kristine's nose)* Will you wake up?

JEAN: *(severely)* Let her sleep!

JULIE: *(sharply)* What?

JEAN: Someone who's been standing over a stove all day has a right to be tired at night. Sleep should be respected. . . .

JULIE: *(changing her tone)* What a considerate thought —it does you credit—you're right, of course. *(holds out her hands to him)* Come out and pick some lilacs for me!

(Kristine goes sleepily to her bedroom. A polka can be heard in the distance.)

JEAN: Go with you?

JULIE: Yes.

JEAN: We can't do that! Absolutely not!

JULIE: I don't understand. *(half-laugh)* Surely you don't imagine . . .

JEAN: No, I don't, but the others might.

JULIE: What? That I've fallen in love with a servant?

JEAN: I'm not a conceited man, but such things happen. And for these people, nothing is sacred.

JULIE: I take it you're moving up in the world!

JEAN: Yes, I am.

JULIE: *(studies him a moment)* And I'm coming down.

JEAN: Don't come down, Miss Julie, take my advice. No one will believe you came down voluntarily. They'll all say you fell.

JULIE: I have a higher opinion of these people than you. Let's see who's right! Come on!

(she stares at him broodingly)

JEAN: You're very strange, do you know that?

JULIE: Perhaps! But then so are you!—For that matter, everything is strange. Life, people, everything. It's all bile drifting, drifting on the water. And then sinking. Sinking. *(pause)* That reminds me of a dream I have now and then. I'm sitting on top of a pillar and can't see how to get down. When I look down I get dizzy. I have to get down, but I don't have the courage to throw myself off. I can't hold on and I'm longing to fall, but I don't fall. I know I won't have any peace until I get down, no rest until I'm down, down to the ground! And if I did get

22

down to the ground, I'd want to go underground. *(pause)* Have you ever felt like that?

JEAN: No. I dream that I'm lying under a tall tree in a dark forest. I want to get up, up to the top, to look out over the bright landscape, where the sun is shining, to rob the bird's nest that's up there of its golden eggs. And I climb and climb, but the trunk is so thick and smooth and it's so far to the first branch. But I know if I just reach that first branch I'll go right to the top just like climbing a ladder. I haven't reached it yet, but someday I will, even if it's only in a dream!

JULIE: *(after a slight pause, in a different tone)* Here we are talking about dreams. Come, let's go out! Just to the park!

JEAN: We must sleep with nine midsummer flowers under our pillow tonight, Miss Julie, and our dreams will come true!

(They turn at the door. Jean raises his hand to his eye.)

JULIE: Did you get something in your eye? Let me see.

JEAN: It's nothing—just a speck of dust—it'll be gone in a minute.

JULIE: My sleeve must have brushed against you. Sit down and let me help you. *(She takes him by the arm and seats him. She tilts his head back and tries to get the speck out with the corner of her handkerchief.)* Sit still, absolutely still! *(slaps his hand)* Didn't you hear me?—Why, you're trembling . . . a big, strong man like you! *(feels his biceps)* With such big arms!

JEAN: *(warning)* Miss Julie!

JULIE: Yes, *Monsieur Jean?*

JEAN: *Attention; je ne suis qu'un homme!*

23

JULIE: Will you sit still! There! Now it's gone! Kiss my hand and thank me.

JEAN: Miss Julie, listen to me! *(rising)* Kristine's gone to bed! Will you listen to me?

JULIE: Kiss my hand first!

JEAN: Listen to me!

JULIE: Kiss my hand first!

JEAN: All right, but you'll have no one to blame but yourself.

JULIE: For what?

JEAN: For what? Are you still a child at twenty-five? Don't you know it's dangerous to play with fire?

JULIE: Not for me. I'm insured.

JEAN: *(boldly)* No, you're not! But even if you were, there's combustible material around that isn't.

JULIE: Meaning you?

JEAN: Yes. Not because it's me, but because I'm young and . . .

JULIE: And irresistibly handsome? What incredible conceit! A Don Juan perhaps? Or a Joseph? Yes, bless my soul, that's it! You're a Joseph!

JEAN: Do you think so?

JULIE: I'm almost afraid of it.

(Jean boldly tries to put his arm around her waist and kiss her. She boxes his ear.)

JULIE: No!

JEAN: Was that serious or joking?

JULIE: Serious.

JEAN: Then you must have been serious a moment ago too. You play much too seriously and that's dangerous. Well, I'm tired of the game. You'll excuse me if I get back to work. The Count will want his boots first thing in the morning and it's long past midnight.

JULIE: Put those boots down!

JEAN: No! It's part of my job, which doesn't include being your plaything. And it never will. It's beneath me.

JULIE: Aren't we proud?

JEAN: In some ways, not others. *(Jean works on a boot)*

JULIE: Have you ever been in love?

JEAN: We don't use that word. But I've been fond of a lot of girls, and once I was sick because I couldn't get the one I wanted. Sick, just like those princes in the *Arabian Nights* who wouldn't eat or drink because of love.

JULIE: Who was she? *(no answer)* Who was she?

JEAN: You can't order me to answer that.

JULIE: But if I ask you as an equal? As a—friend! Who was she?

JEAN: You!

JULIE: *(sits)* How amusing. . . .

JEAN: Yes, I suppose it is. Ridiculous!—That's why I didn't want to tell you about it before. But maybe now I will. *(pause)* Do you know how the world looks from down below?—No, you don't. Neither do hawks and falcons. We can't see their backs because they hover high above us. I grew up in a shack with seven brothers and sisters and a pig, out in the middle of a wasteland where there wasn't even a single tree. But from our window I could see the wall of your father's garden with the tops of the apple trees sticking out over it. It was the Garden of Eden, guarded by angry angels with flaming swords. Nevertheless the other boys and I managed to find our way to the Tree of Life. Now you find me contemptible?

JULIE: Ah! Stealing apples? All boys do that.

JEAN: That's what you say. But you find me contemptible, just the same. Never mind! One day I went into this paradise with my mother, to weed the onion beds. Next to the vegetable patch stood a small Turkish pavilion shaded by jasmine and hung all over with honeysuckle. I couldn't imagine what it was used for, but I knew I'd never seen such a beautiful building. People went in and came out again. Then one day the door was left open. I sneaked in. The walls were covered with pictures of kings and emperors, and the windows had red curtains with tassels on them. Recognize it? The outhouse.

(he breaks off a twig of lilac and holds it for Julie to smell)

I had never been inside the manor outhouse before, never seen anything except the church, but this was more beautiful. No matter what I tried to think about, my thoughts always came back to that place. *(she takes the lilac from him)* And gradually I felt a desire to experience, just for once, the full pleasure of—finally, I sneaked in, looked about, and marveled. And just then I heard someone coming. There was only one way out for the upper class, but for me there was another, a lower one, and I had no choice but to take it.

26

(Julie drops the lilac on the table)

Afterward, I began to run like mad, plunging through the raspberry bushes, plowing through the strawberry patches, until I came upon the rose terrace. There I caught sight of a pink dress and a pair of white stockings. You. I crawled under—well, you can imagine what it was like, under thistles that pricked me and wet dirt that stank to high heaven. And all the while I could see you walking among the roses and said to myself, "If it's true that a thief can enter the kingdom of heaven and be with the angels, then isn't it strange that a poor man's son here on God's green earth can't enter the manor house garden and play with the Count's daughter."

JULIE: *(sentimentally)* Do you think all poor children feel that way?

JEAN: Do all poor . . . yes, of course! Of course!

JULIE: It must be terrible to be poor.

JEAN: Oh, Miss Julie, you don't know. A dog can lie on the sofa with its mistress, a horse may have his nose stroked by the hand of a countess, but a servant . . . *(change of tone)* Of course, now and then you meet somebody with guts enough to move his way up in the world. But how often? Anyway, do you know what I did after that? I threw myself into the millstream with all my clothes on, was pulled out, and got a beating. But the following Sunday, when my father and all the others went to my grandmother's, I arranged to stay home. Then I washed myself all over with soap and warm water, put on my best clothes, and went off to church just to see you once more. After that, I went home determined to die. But I wanted to die beautifully and pleasantly, without pain. I remembered that it was

27

dangerous to sleep under an elderberry bush, and we had a big one that was in full flower. I stripped it of every leaf and blossom, and made a bed of them in the oat bin. Have you ever noticed how smooth oats are? Soft to the touch as human skin. . . . Well, I shut the lid, closed my eyes, and fell asleep. When I woke up I was very ill. But I didn't die, as you can see. What was I trying to prove? I don't know. There was no hope of winning you—you were a symbol of the utter hopelessness of ever getting out of the class into which I was born.

JULIE: *(after a brief pause)* You know, you have a real gift for storytelling. Did you ever go to school?

JEAN: A bit, but I've read a lot of novels and seen a lot of plays. And I've listened to educated people talk—that's where I learned the most.

JULIE: You mean you stand around listening to what we say?

JEAN: Certainly. And I've gotten an earful too, driving the carriage or rowing the boat. One time I heard you and a girlfriend talking . . .

JULIE: Really?—And just what did you hear?

JEAN: Well, I'd better not say. I can tell you I was a little amazed. I couldn't imagine where you had learned such words. Maybe when all's said and done there isn't as much difference between people as we think.

JULIE: Nonsense! The people in my class don't behave like the people in yours do when we're engaged.

JEAN: *(looks at her)* Are you sure?—You don't have to play innocent with me, Miss . . .

JULIE: The man I gave my love to was shit.

JEAN: That's what you all say . . . afterwards.

JULIE: All?

JEAN: I think so. I've heard that phrase used before, on similar occasions.

JULIE: What occasions?

JEAN: The kind we're talking about. I remember the last time I—

JULIE: *(rising)* Oh, stop! I don't want to hear any more!

JEAN: That's interesting—neither did she. Well, if you'll excuse me, I'm going to bed.

JULIE: *(gently)* To bed? On Midsummer Eve?

JEAN: Yes! Dancing with that mob out there doesn't really amuse me.

JULIE: Get the key to the boathouse and row me out on the lake. I want to see the sunrise.

JEAN: Is that wise?

JULIE: Are you worried about your reputation?

JEAN: Why not? Why should I risk looking ridiculous and getting fired, just when I'm trying to establish myself. Besides, I think I owe something to Kristine.

JULIE: So now it's Kristine . . .

JEAN: Yes, but it's you too. Take my advice, go to bed!

JULIE: Since when do you give me orders?

(The peasants are heard singing offstage. Their voices grow louder as they approach.)

JEAN: Just this once, please—for your own sake! It's late. You're tired. You're drunk. You don't know what you're doing! Go to bed! Besides—unless I'm mistaken—I hear the others coming. They'll be looking for me. And if they find us here, you're lost.

PEASANTS: *(under the ensuing dialogue)*
Two ladies came from in the trees,
Tri-di-ri-di ral-la, tri-di-ri-di-ra.
The one was wet below the knees,
Tri-di-ri-di ral la la.

About a lot of wealth they spoke,
Tri-di-ri-di ral-la, tri-di-ri-di-ra.
But truthfully, they both were broke,
Tri-di-ri-di-ral la la.

This wreath of love I give to you.
Tri-di-ri-di ral-la, tri-di-ri-di-ra.
And yet I think of you-know-who,
Tri-di-ri-di ral la la.

JULIE: I know these people. I love them, just as they love me. Let them come. You'll see.

JEAN: No, Miss Julie, they don't love you. They take your food, but they spit on it! Believe me! Listen to them, listen to what they're singing!—No, you'd better not listen!

JULIE: What are they singing?

JEAN: It's a nasty song! About you and me.

JULIE: Damn! Those cowards!

JEAN: A mob is always cowardly! You can't fight them, you can only run away!

JULIE: Run away? Where? We can't get out—and we can't go into Kristine's room.

JEAN: True. But there's my room. Necessity knows no rules. Besides, you can trust me. I'm your friend, your true, loyal, respectful friend.

JULIE: But suppose—suppose they look for you in there?

JEAN: I'll bolt the door. If they break it down, I'll shoot!—Come! *(She hesitates. Jean is on his knees.)* Please!

JULIE: *(urgently)* Do you promise me that . . . ?

JEAN: I swear!

(Miss Julie runs off right. Jean hastens after her. Led by a fiddler, the servants and farm people enter, dressed festively, with flowers in their hats. On the table they place a small barrel of beer and a keg of liquor, both garlanded. Glasses are brought out, and the drinking starts. A dance circle is formed and "Two Ladies Came from in the Trees" is sung. When the dance is finished, everyone leaves, singing.)

(Miss Julie enters alone. She notices the mess in the kitchen, wrings her hands, then takes out her powder puff and powders her nose. Jean enters excited and in high spirits.)

JEAN: There, you see? You heard them. Do you still think that it's possible for us to stay here?

JULIE: No, I don't. But what can we do?

JEAN: Leave, travel, far away from here.

JULIE: Travel? But where to?

JEAN: Switzerland. The Italian lakes. Ever been there?

JULIE: No. Is it beautiful?

JEAN: An eternal summer—oranges, laurel trees . . . incredible!

JULIE: But what'll we do there?

JEAN: I'll open a hotel—with first-class service for first-class people.

JULIE: Hotel?

JEAN: That's the life for me. Always new faces, new languages. No time to worry or be nervous. No looking for something to do—there's always work to be done. Day and night bells ringing, train whistles blowing, carriages coming and going, and the money keeps rolling in! That's the life for me!

JULIE: Yes, for *you*. But what about me?

JEAN: You'll be mistress of the house, the jewel in our crown! With your looks . . . and your personality—success is guaranteed! It'll be wonderful! You'll sit in your office like a queen, setting your slaves in motion by pressing a button. The guests will timidly file past your throne and lay their offerings at your feet.—You have no idea how people cower when they get their bill.—I'll salt the bills and you'll sugar them with your prettiest smile.—Come on, let's get out of here right away!—*(takes a timetable out of his pocket)* We'll go, we'll take a train, a ship, we'll get there by . . . let me see . . .

JULIE: That's all very well. But Jean—you have to give me strength—Tell me you love me! Put your arms around me!

JEAN: *(reluctantly)* I want to—but I don't dare. Not again in this house, not again. I love you—never doubt that. You don't doubt it, do you, Miss Julie?

JULIE: "Miss!"—Call me Julie! There are no barriers between us any more. Call me Julie!

JEAN: I can't! There'll always be barriers between us as long as we stay in this house.—There's the past and there's the Count. I've never met anyone I feel so much respect for—I just have to see his gloves lying on a chair and I feel small—I just have to hear that bell ring and I jump like a skittish horse—when I see his boots standing there so straight and proud, my back starts to bow. *(kicking the boots)* Superstitions and prejudices we learned as children! But they can be forgotten. I just need to get to another country, a different place, and people will crawl on their hands and knees when they see my uniform—*they'll* be on their hands and knees, not me! I wasn't born to crawl. I've got guts, I've got character, and once I reach that first branch, you watch me climb! I'm a servant today, but next year I'll own my own hotel. In ten years I'll have enough to retire. Then I'll go to Rumania, get myself decorated, and could—mind you I said *could*—end up a count!

JULIE: How nice for you.

JEAN: In Rumania you can buy yourself a title, so you'll be a countess after all. *My* countess!

JULIE: But I don't care about that—I'm leaving all that behind. Tell me you love me, otherwise what does it matter what I am?

JEAN: I'll tell you a thousand times—later. Not here! Above all, let's keep our feelings out of this or we'll make a mess of everything! We have to look at this calmly, like sensible people. *(he takes out a cigar, snips the end, and lights it)* You sit there, and I'll sit here. We'll talk as if nothing had happened.

33

JULIE: God, don't you have any feelings?

JEAN: Nobody has more, but I've learned to control them.

JULIE: You were kissing my shoe, and now—

JEAN: *(harshly)* That was then. Now we have other things to think about.

JULIE: Don't be so mean!

JEAN: I'm not! But why don't you use your head? What we've done is madness. Let's not do it again. The count could come back at any minute, and we've got to decide what to do with our lives before he does. What do you think of my plans for the future? Do you approve?

JULIE: They sound reasonable. But just one question: for such a big undertaking you need capital—do you have it?

JEAN: *(chewing on the cigar)* Certainly! I have my professional expertise, my wide experience, and my knowledge of languages. That's capital enough, I should think!

JULIE: But you can't buy a train ticket with it.

JEAN: That's true. That's why I need a partner to get me the money.

JULIE: Where can you find one right now?

JEAN: You must get it, if you want to be my partner.

JULIE: I can't. I don't own anything myself.

JEAN: *(after a pause)* Then the whole thing's off.

JULIE: And . . . ?

JEAN: Things will stay as they are.

JULIE: Do you think I'm going to stay in this house as your mistress? With all the servants pointing their fingers at me? Do you think I can face my father after this? No! Take me away from here, away from the shame and dishonor! My God, my God! What have I done! *(she cries)*

JEAN: So that's the tune now, is it? What have you done? The same as many before you.

JULIE: *(screams convulsively)* And now you hate me!— I'm falling, I'm falling!

JEAN: Fall as far as me and I'll lift you up again.

JULIE: What terrible power drew me to you? The weak to the strong? The falling to the rising? Or was it love? This—love? Do you know what love is?

JEAN: Do I? You bet I do! Do you think I never had a girl before?

JULIE: The things you say, the thoughts you think!

JEAN: That's what I've learned, and that's who I am! Don't be so nervous and don't act so high and mighty. You're no better than me now! So be a good girl and come over here. I'll pour you a glass of something special!
(he opens a drawer in the table, takes out a wine bottle, and fills two glasses already used)

JULIE: Where did you get that wine?

JEAN: From the wine cellar.

JULIE: My father's burgundy!

JEAN: Should be good enough for his son-in-law.

JULIE: And I drank beer!

JEAN: That only shows your taste is worse than mine.

35

JULIE: Thief!

JEAN: You gonna squeal on me?

JULIE: Oh God! Partner in crime with a petty thief! Was I drunk? Have I been walking in my sleep? Midsummer Eve! A time of innocent fun!

JEAN: Innocent, eh?

JULIE: *(pacing back and forth)* Is there anyone on earth more miserable than I am?

JEAN: Why *should* you be? After such a conquest? Think of Kristine in there. Don't you think she has feelings too?

JULIE: I did, but not anymore. No, a servant is a servant. . . .

JEAN: And a whore is a whore!

JULIE: *(on her knees, her hands clasped)* Oh, God in Heaven, end my miserable life! Lift me out of the filth I'm sinking in. Save me! Save me!

a prayer

JEAN: I have to admit it, I feel sorry for you. When I was lying in the onion beds, looking up at you on the rose terrace, well . . . I might as well tell you. I had the same dirty thoughts as any other boy.

JULIE: But you wanted to die for me!

JEAN: In the oat bin? That was just talk.

JULIE: You mean a lie?

JEAN: *(beginning to feel sleepy, he yawns)* More or less! I got the idea from a newspaper story about a chimney sweep who curled up in a firewood bin full of lilacs because he'd been sued for not paying his child support. . . .

JULIE: So this is what you're really like?

36

JEAN: I had to think of something. It's the fancy talk that catches the women.

JULIE: You're scum!

JEAN: You're shit!

JULIE: So now you've seen the falcon's back. . . .

JEAN: Not exactly its *back*. . . .

JULIE: And I was to be the first branch. . . .

JEAN: But the branch was rotten. . . .

JULIE: I was to be the window dressing for your hotel. . . .

JEAN: And I the hotel. . . .

JULIE: Sit at your desk, entice your customers, pad their bills. . . .

JEAN: That I'd do myself. . . .

JULIE: How can a human soul be so filthy?

JEAN: Then go take a bath!

JULIE: You lackey, you menial, stand up when I talk to you!

JEAN: Lackey's harlot, menial's whore, shut up and get out of here! Who are you to lecture me on coarseness? None of my kind is ever as coarse as you were tonight. Have you ever seen one of your own maids throw herself at a man the way you did? Have you ever seen any girl of my class asking for it like that? I've only seen it among animals and whores.

JULIE: *(crushed)* You're right. Hurt me, walk all over me. I don't deserve any better. I'm worthless. But help me! If you see any way out at all, help me, Jean, please!

37

JEAN: *(more gently)* I'd be doing myself a disservice if I denied my share in this seduction. But do you think someone in my position would have dared even to look at you if you hadn't asked for it? I'm still amazed. . . .

JULIE: And proud. . . .

JEAN: Why not? Though I must say it was a little too easy to be very exciting.

JULIE: Go on, hurt me some more!

JEAN: *(rising)* No! I'm sorry I said that. I never hit somebody who's down—least of all a woman. On the one hand, I can't deny I'm pleased to find out that what I saw glittering up above was only fool's gold, that the falcon's back was only as gray as its belly, that the lovely complexion was only powder, that there could be grime under the manicured nails, and that a dirty handkerchief is still dirty, even if it smells of perfume . . . ! On the other hand, it hurts to find out that what I was striving for wasn't finer, more substantial. It hurts to see you sink far lower than your own cook. It hurts like watching the last flowers of summer beaten down by autumn rains and turned to muck.

JULIE: You talk as if you were already above me.

JEAN: I am. I can make you a countess, but you can never make me a count.

JULIE: My father is a count. You can never have that!

JEAN: True. But I can be the father of counts, if—

JULIE: You're a thief. I'm not.

JEAN: There are worse things than being a thief! A lot worse. Besides, when I come into a family, I consider myself almost like one of the children. And

38

you don't call it stealing when a child snatches a berry off a bush full of fruit. *(his passion is aroused again)* Miss Julie, you're a glorious woman, much too good for the likes of me! You were drinking and you lost your head. Now you want to cover up your mistake by telling yourself that you love me! You don't. Maybe there was a physical attraction— in which case your kind of love is no better than mine.—But I could never be satisfied to be just an animal to you, and I could never arouse real love in you.

JULIE: How do you know that for sure?

JEAN: You mean there's a chance?—Oh, I could fall in love with you, no doubt about it. You're beautiful, you're refined—*(approaching and taking her hand)* cultured, lovable when you want to be, and the fire you start in a man isn't likely to go out. *(putting his arm about her waist)* You're like hot wine filled with spices, and one of your kisses is enough to . . . *(he tries to lead her out, but she slowly frees herself)*

JULIE: Let me go!—You won't get me that way.

JEAN: *How* then?—Not like that? Not with caresses and pretty speeches? Not with plans about the future or rescue from disgrace? *How* then?

JULIE: How? How? I don't know!—No way at all!—I hate you like I hate rats, but I can't escape you.

JEAN: Escape *with* me!

JULIE: Escape? *(pulling herself together)* Yes, we must escape! But I'm so tired. Give me a glass of wine. *(Jean pours the wine. She looks at her watch.)* We need to talk first. We still have a little time. *(she drains the glass, then holds it out for more)*

JEAN: Don't drink so much. You'll get drunk.

JULIE: What difference does it make?

JEAN: What difference? It looks cheap! What did you want to tell me?

JULIE: We must escape! But we'll talk first. I mean I'll talk. So far you've done all the talking. You've told me about your life, now I'll tell you about mine, so we'll know all about each other before we go off together.

JEAN: Excuse me a minute. Are you sure you won't regret this afterwards, revealing your secrets to me?

JULIE: Aren't you my friend?

JEAN: Sometimes. But don't count on it.

JULIE: You don't mean that. Besides, everybody knows my secrets anyway. *(pause)* Listen. My mother was a commoner, from a very humble background. She was brought up believing in equality of the sexes, women's rights and all that. The idea of marriage repelled her. So when my father proposed, she said she'd never marry him, but that he could be her lover. He insisted he didn't want the woman he loved to be less respected than he was, but she said she didn't care what the world thought, and, believing he couldn't live without her, he accepted her conditions. But now his friends avoided him, and his life was restricted to taking care of the estate, which couldn't satisfy him. I came into the world against my mother's wishes, as far as I can tell. I was left to run wild, and on top of that I had to learn everything a boy learns, so that I could be living proof that a woman is just as good as a man. I had to wear boys' clothes, I was taught to take care of horses, but I was never allowed to milk cows. I had to groom and harness and go hunting. I even had to watch them slaughter animals. It was

40

disgusting! All the men on the estate were given the women's jobs, and all the women the men's jobs, until the whole place became run down and we became the laughingstock of the district. Finally my father came out of his trance and rebelled. He changed everything and ran the place his way. My parents were married very quietly. Then my mother got sick. I don't know what was wrong, but she had convulsions, hid in the attic and the garden, and some nights she didn't come home at all. Then came the big fire that you've heard about. The house, the stables, and the barns burned to the ground under circumstances that suggested arson. The accident happened the day after the insurance had expired. The quarterly payment my father had sent in was delayed because of a messenger's carelessness, so it didn't get there in time. *(she refills her own glass and drinks)*

JEAN: You've had enough.

JULIE: Who cares? We were destitute and had to sleep in the carriages. My father didn't know where to get money to rebuild. He had neglected his old friends, so they had forgotten him. Then my mother suggested that he borrow from a childhood friend of hers, a brick manufacturer who lived nearby. My father got the loan without having to pay interest, which surprised him. So the estate was rebuilt. *(drinks)* Do you know who started the fire?

JEAN: The Countess, your mother.

JULIE: Do you know who the brick manufacturer was?

JEAN: Your mother's lover?

JULIE: Do you know whose money it was?

JEAN: Uh, wait a minute. *(pause)* I give up.

JULIE: It was my mother's.

JEAN: You mean the Count's—unless they didn't sign an agreement when they got married.

JULIE: They didn't. My mother had a small inheritance which she didn't want under my father's control, so she entrusted it to her—friend.

JEAN: Who stole it!

JULIE: Exactly. He kept it. Well, my father found out what had happened, but he couldn't bring it to court, couldn't repay his wife's lover, couldn't prove it was his wife's money! It was my mother's revenge for being forced to marry against her will. He almost killed himself. There was a rumor that he tried to shoot himself, but failed. He managed to go on living, and my mother had to suffer for what she'd done. Imagine what those five years were like for me! I loved my father, but I sided with my mother because I didn't know the facts. I learned from her to hate men. You know she hated the whole male sex, and I swore to her that I'd never be a slave to any man.

JEAN: But you got engaged to that lawyer.

JULIE: In order to make him my slave.

JEAN: And he wasn't willing?

JULIE: He was willing, all right, but I didn't give him the chance. I got tired of him.

JEAN: Is that what I saw in the stable yard?

JULIE: What did you see?

JEAN: How he broke off the engagement. You can still see it!

JULIE: That's a lie. I was the one who broke it off. Did he say that he did? That scum.

JEAN: Scum? I don't think so! You hate men, Miss?

JULIE: Yes . . . most of the time. But when the weakness comes, it's a burning that will never stop, never leave me alone! Damn it!

JEAN: So you hate me too?

JULIE: Beyond words. I'd like to have you put to death like an animal.

JEAN: Ah, the penalty for bestiality—the criminal gets two years' hard labor, and the animal is put to death. Right?

JULIE: Right.

JEAN: But there's no criminal here—and no animal. So what'll we do?

JULIE: Leave!

JEAN: To make life hell for each other?

JULIE: No, to enjoy ourselves for a day or two, a week, for as long as we can, and then—to die. . . .

JEAN: Die? That's stupid! It's better to open a hotel.

JULIE: *(as if she hadn't heard)* . . . on the shores of Lake Como, where the sun is always shining, where the laurels are green at Christmas and the golden oranges glow. . . .

JEAN: Lake Como is a stinking wet hole, and the only oranges I ever saw there were in the grocery stores! But it's a good tourist spot. There are plenty of villas to be rented out to lovers. Now *that's* a profitable business! You know why? They sign a lease for six months, and they leave after three weeks.

JULIE: Why after three weeks?

JEAN: Because that's just about as long as they can stand each other. But they still have to pay the rent in full. . . . Then you can rent it out again to another couple, and so on! There's no shortage of love, even though it doesn't last very long.

JULIE: You don't want to die with me?

JEAN: I don't want to die at all. For one thing, I like living. For another, I think suicide is a sin against the Providence that gave us life.

JULIE: You believe in God?

JEAN: Of course I do. And I go to church every other Sunday. Look, I'm sick of all this. I'm going to bed.

JULIE: Are you! You think you're going to get off that easy? A man owes something to the woman he's ruined.

JEAN: *(throws her a change purse)* Here! I don't like owing anybody anything!

JULIE: *(pretending not to notice)* Do you know what the law says?

JEAN: Unfortunately the law doesn't say anything about a woman who seduces a man.

JULIE: Do you see any way out, other than going away, getting married, and getting divorced?

JEAN: Suppose I refuse such a bad match?

JULIE: Bad match?

JEAN: Yes. For me. I've got better ancestors than you. There's no arsonist in my family!

JULIE: How do you *know*?

44

JEAN: You can't prove otherwise because we don't keep charts on our ancestors, except for the police records. But I've seen your family tree in that book on the drawing room table. Do you know who the mother was? Do you know who the founding father was? A miller who let the king sleep with his wife one night [during the Danish war]! I don't have any noble ancestors like that! I don't have any noble ancestors at all, but I could become one myself.

JULIE: This is what I get for confiding in someone unworthy, for sacrificing my family's honor!

JEAN: Dishonor, you mean! Well, I told you so. One shouldn't drink, because then one talks. And one shouldn't talk.

JULIE: Oh, how I regret it! If only you loved me at least!

JEAN: For the last time—what are you talking about? Should I cry? Jump over your riding crop? Kiss you and lure you off to Lake Como for three weeks, and then . . . What am I supposed to do? What do you want? This is getting painful, but that's what I get for messing around with women. Miss Julie, I see that you're unhappy. I know you're suffering, but I can't understand you. My people don't behave like this. We don't hate each other like this. We make love for fun when we get time off from work, but we don't have all day and night like you do! I think you're sick, really sick. Your mother was crazy and her ideas have poisoned your life!

JULIE: So be kind to me. At least now you're talking like a human being!

JEAN: Be human yourself. You can spit on me, but I can't wipe it on you.

JULIE: Help me, Jean. Help me! Just tell me what to do, where to go.

JEAN: Christ! As if I knew.

JULIE: I've been insane, driven by lust, but does that mean there's no way out?

JEAN: Stay here and keep calm. Nobody knows anything.

JULIE: Impossible! The people here know. Kristine knows!

JEAN: They don't know a thing. Anyhow, they'd never believe it.

JULIE: *(hesitantly)* But—it could happen again.

JEAN: That's true.

JULIE: And the consequences?

JEAN: *(panicked)* Consequences? Why didn't I think about that? There's only one thing to do. Leave, right away! I can't go with you, that would give us away, so you have to go alone. Abroad. Anywhere.

JULIE: Alone? Where? I can't do that!

JEAN: You have to. And before the Count gets back. If you stay, we both know what'll happen. Once you make a mistake, you want to keep doing it since the damage has already been done. You get more and more careless, until you're caught! So go! Later you can write to the Count and confess everything—except that it was me. He'll never guess—and I don't think he'll be real anxious to find out!

JULIE: I'll go if you come with me.

JEAN: Are you crazy, woman? "Miss Julie Runs Away with Her Servant"—in two days it would be in the

46

newspapers. The Count would never live through
it!

JULIE: I can't go, I can't stay. Help me! I'm so tired, so
terribly tired. Order me! Set me in motion. I can't
think or act on my own.

JEAN: What miserable creatures you people are! What
gives you the right to strut around with your noses
in the air, as if you owned the world? All right, I'll
order you. Go upstairs and get dressed, get some
money for the trip, and then come back down!

JULIE: *(softly)* Come up with me.

JEAN: To your room? You're going crazy again! *(pause)*
No! Go right now!

JULIE: Don't be so mean, Jean.

JEAN: Orders always sound mean. Now you know how
it feels.

*(Miss Julie exits. Left alone, Jean sighs with relief. He sits
at the table, takes out a notebook and pencil, and begins
adding up figures, counting aloud as he works. He continues until Kristine enters, dressed for church. She is carrying a white tie and shirt front.)*

KRISTINE: Lord Jesus, what a mess! What have you
been up to?

JEAN: It was Miss Julie. She dragged the whole crowd
in here. You must have been sleeping soundly if
you didn't hear anything.

KRISTINE: I slept like a log.

JEAN: Dressed for church already?

KRISTINE: Yes indeed? You promised to go to Commu-
nion with me today, remember?

47

JEAN: Oh yes, that's right. And you brought my things. All right, put it on me!

(He sits down. Kristine starts to put on his shirt front and tie.)

JEAN: What's the text for today?

KRISTINE: On St. John's Day? The beheading of John the Baptist, what else?

JEAN: God, that will go on forever. Hey, you're choking me! Oh, am I ever tired!

KRISTINE: What were you doing up all night? You look absolutely green.

JEAN: I've been sitting here gabbing with Miss Julie.

KRISTINE: That girl, she doesn't know how to behave herself.

JEAN: *(after a pause)* You know, Kristine . . .

KRISTINE: What?

JEAN: It's really strange, when you think about it. Her, I mean.

KRISTINE: What's so strange?

JEAN: Everything.

(Pause. Kristine sees the half-empty glasses on the table.)

KRISTINE: Were you drinking with her?

JEAN: Yes.

KRISTINE: Shame on you. *(change of tone)* Look me in the eye.

JEAN: Yes.

KRISTINE: Is it possible? Is it *possible?*

48

JEAN: Yes, it is.

KRISTINE: Ugh! I never would have believed it! *(she shudders audibly)*

JEAN: You're not jealous of her, are you?

KRISTINE: No, not of her! If it had been Clara or Sophie, I'd have scratched your eyes out. But her? That's different. I don't know why—it just is. But it's still disgusting!

JEAN: Are you angry with her then?

KRISTINE: No. At you. You were mean and cruel to do a thing like that! Very mean. The poor girl! Oh, I don't care who knows it, I won't stay in this house any longer! Not when I can't respect the people I work for.

JEAN: Why do you want to respect them?

KRISTINE: You're so clever, you tell me! Do you want to wait on people who aren't respectable? Do you? If you ask me, you'd be disgracing yourself.

JEAN: At least it's a comfort to know they aren't any better than we are.

KRISTINE: No, I don't think so. If they're not any better, there's nothing to strive for. And think of the Count! Think of him. As if he hasn't had enough misery in his life! Lord Jesus! No, I won't stay in this house any longer. And it had to be with someone like you! If it had been that lawyer, if it had been somebody better . . .

JEAN: Now just a minute—

KRISTINE: I know, I know—you're all right for what you are. But there's still a difference between people and *people*. No, I'll never be able to forget this

49

business with Miss Julie! She was so proud and so aloof toward men, you'd never believe she'd go and throw herself at one—especially at someone like you! And she was going to have Diana shot for going after the gatekeeper's mutt. Well, let me tell you! I won't stay here any longer. On the 24th of October, I quit!

JEAN: And then?

KRISTINE: Well, since you mention it, it's about time you looked for something else, since we're going to get married.

JEAN: What would I look for? If I'm married, I can't get a job like this.

KRISTINE: Well, I know that. But you could get a job as a porter, or try for a job as a caretaker in some government office. The wages are low but the benefits are good, and there's a pension for the widow and children.

JEAN: That's all well and good, but it's not my style to start thinking about dying for wife and children. My ambitions are a little higher than that!

KRISTINE: You and your ambitions! What about your obligations? You'd better start thinking about them.

JEAN: Don't start nagging me about my obligations. I know what I have to do. Anyway, we have plenty of time to work this out. Go and get ready and we'll go to church.

KRISTINE: Who's that wandering around up there?

JEAN: I don't know—maybe it's Clara.

KRISTINE: *(going)* Do you suppose the Count came back without our hearing him?

JEAN: *(scared)* The Count? No, it can't be. He'd have rung!

KRISTINE: Well, God help us! I've never seen anything like this before!

(Kristine exits. The sun has risen and shines through the treetops in the park. The light shifts gradually until it slants in through the windows. Jean goes to the door and signals. Miss Julie enters, dressed in traveling clothes and carrying a small bird cage, covered with cloth, which she places on a chair.)

JULIE: I'm ready.

JEAN: Shhhh! Kristine is awake.

JULIE: *(agitated)* Does she suspect something?

JEAN: She doesn't know anything. My God, you look awful!

JULIE: Why? What's wrong?

JEAN: You're pale as a ghost, and pardon me for saying so—your face is dirty.

JULIE: Well, I'll wash it. *(she goes to the sink and washes her face and hands)* Give me a towel. Oh! The sun is rising!

JEAN: And so the demons disappear.

JULIE: Yes. The ones that possessed us last night. *(pause)* Jean, listen. Come with me . . . I have some money now.

JEAN: *(skeptically)* Enough?

JULIE: Enough for a start. Come with me. I can't travel alone today. Midsummer Day on a stuffy train, packed in with crowds of people who'll be staring at me, stopping at every station, when I'd rather

51

be flying! I can't, I can't! And the memories will come—memories of Midsummer Day when I was a child: the church decorated with birch leaves and lilacs, dinner at the big table with relatives and friends, the afternoon in the park, with dancing, music, flowers, and games. No matter how hard we try to run away, the memories always follow in the baggage car . . . along with the shame and guilt!

JEAN: All right, I'll go with you. But it has to be right now, right away, before it's too late!

JULIE: *(picking up bird cage)* Get dressed then.

JEAN: But no baggage! It would give us away.

JULIE: No, nothing! Only what we can have in the compartment.

JEAN: What have you got there? What is that?

JULIE: It's only my canary. I don't want to leave her behind!

JEAN: What? Bring a bird cage with us? You're crazy! Put it down.

JULIE: It's the only thing I'm taking from my home. The only living thing that likes me since Diana was unfaithful to me. Don't be cruel! Let me take it.

JEAN: Put the cage down, I said. And don't talk so loud. Kristine will hear us.

JULIE: No, I won't leave her in the hands of strangers! I'd rather you killed her!

JEAN: Bring it here, then. I'll cut its head off.

JULIE: Yes, but don't hurt it! No, I can't!

JEAN: Bring it here! I can!

(Julie takes the bird from the cage and kisses it)

JULIE: Dear little Serena, are you going to die and leave your mistress?

JEAN: Please don't make a scene. Your whole future is at stake! Hurry up!

(He snatches the bird from her, puts it on the board, and picks up a meat cleaver. Julie turns away.)

You should have learned how to slaughter chickens instead of how to shoot pistols. *(he chops off the bird's head)* Then you wouldn't feel faint at the sight of blood.

JULIE: *(screaming)* Kill me too! Kill me! You can slaughter an innocent creature without blinking an eye! I hate you! I despise you! There's blood between us. I curse the moment I saw you! I curse the moment I came to life in my mother's womb!

JEAN: What good does cursing do? Let's go.

JULIE: *(going to chopping block)* No, I don't want to go yet. I can't! I have to see! Shhh! There's a carriage out there. . . . *(she listens without taking her eyes off the chopping block)* You don't think I can stand the sight of blood. You think I'm so weak. Oh, I'd like to see your blood, your brains on a chopping block! I'd like to see all of you swimming in a sea of blood! I could drink out of your skull, bathe my feet in your open chest, and eat your heart roasted whole! You think I'm weak. You think I love you because my womb craved your seed! You think I want to carry your spawn under my heart and feed it with my blood—bear your child and take your name! Listen, you—what is your family name? I've never heard it! I bet you don't have one! I'd have to be "Mrs. Shack" or "Madam Shit Pile"! You dog with my name on your collar; you lackey with my crest on your buttons! I share you with my cook! I'm my own servant's rival! Oh! Oh! Oh! You think I'm a coward who'll run away. No! I'm staying—*no matter what!* My father will come home, find his desk broken open, his money gone. Then he'll ring that bell—twice for his valet—and then he'll send for the police—and I'll tell everything! Everything! Oh, what a relief to have an end to it all! A real end. . . . Then my father will have a stroke and die, and that'll be the end of all of us. There will be calm . . . peace . . . eternal rest! The coat of arms will be broken against his coffin, the Count's line will be extinct, but the valet's line will continue in an orphanage, win its laurels in the gutter, and end in jail!

JEAN: There speaks the noble blood! Bravo, Miss Julie. Just don't let that miller out of the bag!

(Kristine enters, dressed for church, with a psalm book in her hand. Julie rushes to her as if for protection.)

JULIE: Help me, Kristine! Help me against this man!

KRISTINE: *(coldly)* What a fine way to behave on a Sunday morning! *(she looks at the chopping block)* And look at this mess. What does all this mean? I never heard such yelling and screaming!

JULIE: Kristine, you're a woman, you're my friend! Beware of this man, he's evil!

JEAN: While you ladies are talking things over, I think I'll go in and shave. *(he exits)*

JULIE: You've got to listen to me! You've got to understand!

KRISTINE: No, I could never understand such loose ways! Where are you off to in your traveling clothes—and what was he doing with his hat on? Well? Well?

54

JULIE: Listen to me, Kristine. Listen and I'll tell you everything!

KRISTINE: I don't want to know anything!

JULIE: You must listen to me!

KRISTINE: Listen to what? Is it about the shenanigans with Jean? Well, you see, I couldn't care less. It's none of my business. But if you're trying to trick him into running away with you, well, I'll put a stop to that!

JULIE: Calm down, Kristine, and listen to me! I can't stay here, and Jean can't stay here—so we have to go away.

KRISTINE: Hm, hm, hm!

JULIE: Wait, I've got an idea!—All three of us can go away—together—to Switzerland, and start a hotel! —I have money, you see!—Jean and I would be responsible for the whole thing—and you—I thought—could run the kitchen! . . . Doesn't that sound wonderful?—Say you'll come, Kristine, and everything will be settled!—Say yes! Please! *(Julie embraces Kristine and pats her)*

KRISTINE: Hm, hm.

JULIE: *(presto tempo)* You've never been traveling, Kristine.—You have to get out and see the world! You can't imagine how much fun it is to travel by train —constantly, new faces, new countries!—We'll go to Hamburg and take a look at the zoo.—You'll love that!—And we'll go to the theatre and the opera—and then when we get to Munich we'll have the museums. There are Rubenses and Raphaels, those great painters, as you know.— You've heard of Munich, where King Ludwig lived.—You know, the king who went insane.—And

55

we'll see his castle.—It's still there, and it looks just like the ones in fairy tales!—And from there it isn't far to Switzerland—with the Alps!—Imagine, the Alps have snow in the middle of summer!—And oranges grow there, and laurel trees that are green the whole year round!

(Jean can be seen in the wings right, sharpening his razor on a strop which he holds with his teeth and his left hand. He listens to the conversation with satisfaction, nodding now and then in approval. Julie continues tempo prestissimo.)

—And that's where we'll open a hotel.—I'll be at the desk while Jean greets the guests . . . goes out shopping . . . writes letters.—That's the life, I'm telling you.—Train whistles blowing, carriages arriving, bells ringing in the rooms and down in the restaurant—and I'll make out the bills—and I can salt them! You'll never believe how timid travelers are when they have to pay their bills. And you— you'll be the lady of the kitchen!—Naturally, you won't be standing over the stove yourself—and you'll have to dress nicely and neatly since people will see you.—And with your looks!—I'm not flattering you—one fine day you'll catch yourself a man! A rich Englishman, you'll see.—Those people are so easy to *(slowing down)* catch!—And we'll be rich!—We'll build a villa on Lake Como!—Of course—it rains—a little bit—there—sometimes— but—the sun has to shine once in a while—even though it's usually dark—and then—or else—we can go home—and come back—here—or—somewhere else. . . .

KRISTINE: Listen to me! Do you believe any of that yourself, Miss Julie?

JULIE: *(beside herself)* Do I believe it?

KRISTINE: Yes!

JULIE: *(sighs)* I don't know. I don't believe in anything anymore. . . . Nothing. Nothing at all. *(she sinks her head in her arms on the table)*

KRISTINE: *(turning to where Jean is standing)* So, you were planning to run away, were you?

JEAN: *(disconcerted, putting razor on the table)* We weren't exactly going to run away. Don't exaggerate. You heard Miss Julie's plan! Even if she's tired after being up all night, it's still a practical plan.

KRIST'NE: Listen to him! Did you think I'd be the kitchen wench for that . . .

JEAN: You watch what you say in front of your mistress! Understand?

KRISTINE: Mistress?

JEAN: Yes!

KRISTINE: Listen! Listen to him!

JEAN: Yes, you listen! That's what you need to do—and talk a little less! Miss Julie is your mistress. If you despise her for what she's done, you should despise yourself for the same reason!

KRISTINE: I've always held myself high enough—

JEAN: To be able to look down on other people!

KRISTINE: —to keep from doing anything that's beneath me! You can't say that the Count's cook has been up to something with the stable groom, or the swineherd, can you?

JEAN: No. You've had yourself a gentleman, lucky you!

KRISTINE: Yes, a gentleman who sells the oats from the Count's stable!

JEAN: You should talk! Taking a payoff from the grocer and bribes from the butcher!

KRISTINE: What?

JEAN: And you can't respect your employers. You! *You!*

KRISTINE: Are you coming to church with me now? You could use a good sermon after your fine deed!

JEAN: No. I'm not going to church today! Go by yourself and confess your sins!

KRISTINE: Yes, I'll do just that—and I'll bring back enough forgiveness for you too! The Savior suffered and died on the cross for all our sins, and if we go to him with faith and a penitent heart, he will take all our sins upon himself.

JEAN: Does that include the groceries?

JULIE: *(who has been half-listening to this last exchange)* Do you really believe that, Kristine?

KRISTINE: It's my living faith, as sure as I'm standing here. It's the faith I learned as a child, Miss Julie, and kept ever since. "Where sin aboundeth, grace aboundeth also!"

JULIE: If only I had your faith. If only . . .

KRISTINE: Well, you see, you can't get that without God's special grace, and that isn't given to just anyone—

JULIE: Who gets it then?

KRISTINE: That's the great secret of the workings of grace, Miss Julie, and God is no respecter of persons. With him the last shall be the first—

JULIE: Then he does respect the last.

KRISTINE: —and it is easier for a camel to go through the eye of a needle than for a rich man to enter the Kingdom of God. That's the way it is, Miss Julie! Anyhow, I'm going now—alone, and on my way out I'm going to tell the stable groom not to let any horses out, in case anyone has any ideas about leaving before the Count gets back!—Goodbye! *(she exits)*

JEAN: What a witch! *(pause)* And all this because of a canary.

JULIE: *(wearily)* Never mind the canary. Can you see any way out of this, any end to it?

JEAN: *(after a long pause)* No.

JULIE: What would you do if you were in my place?

JEAN: In your place? Let me see. An aristocrat, a woman, who's—fallen. I don't know—or maybe I do.

JULIE: *(picking up razor and making a gesture of cutting her throat)* Like this?

JEAN: Yes! But I wouldn't do it, you understand! That's the difference between us!

JULIE: Because you're a man and I'm a woman? What difference does that make?

JEAN: Just the difference—between man and woman.

JULIE: *(looking at the razor)* I want to. But I can't! My father couldn't either, the time he should have.

JEAN: No, he was right not to! He had to get his revenge first.

JULIE: And now my mother is revenged again, through me.

JEAN: Didn't you ever love your father, Miss Julie?

59

JULIE: Oh yes, deeply, but I must have hated him too. I must have without even realizing it! But he's the one who brought me up to despise my own sex, to be half woman and half man. Who's to blame for what happened? My father, my mother, myself? Myself? I don't have a self! I don't have a thought I didn't get from my father, an emotion I didn't get from my mother, and the last—that all people are equal—I got from my fiancé. That's why I say he's scum! How can it be my fault? Should I blame Jesus, the way Kristine does? No, I'm too proud— and too sensible—thanks to what my father taught me. As for someone rich not getting into heaven, that's a lie. But at least Kristine won't get in—how will she explain the money she has in the bank? Who's to blame? What difference does it make? I'm still the one who has to take on the guilt, face the consequences. . . .

JEAN: Yes, but— *(There are two sharp rings on the bell. Julie jumps to her feet. Jean puts on his livery.)*

JEAN: The Count is back! What if Kristine . . . *(Jean goes to the speaking tube, presses it and listens)*

JULIE: What if he's been to his desk?

JEAN: This is Jean. . . . Yes, sir. . . . Yes, sir. Right away, sir . . . in half an hour.

JULIE: *(panicked)* What did he say? For God's sake, what did he say?

JEAN: He wants his boots and his coffee in half an hour.

JULIE: Then there's half an hour. . . . Oh, I'm so tired! I can't do anything. Can't regret, can't think, can't run, can't stay, can't live—can't die. Help me. Order me, and I'll obey like a dog. Do me this last

60

service—save my honor, save his name. You know what I should do, but don't have the will to do. You must will it and order me to do it!

JEAN: I don't know—I can't either—not now. I don't know why. It's like this coat made it happen.—I can't order you.—And now, since the Count talked to me—I—I can't really explain it—but—ah, it's the damn lackey in me! If the Count came down here now—and ordered me to cut my throat, I'd do it on the spot.

JULIE: Then pretend you're him, and I'm you! You gave such a good performance before when you knelt at my feet.—You were a real nobleman.— Or—have you ever seen a hypnotist? *(Jean nods)* He says to his subject, "Take this broom," and he takes it. He says, "Sweep," and he sweeps. . . .

JEAN: But the subject has to be asleep.

JULIE: *(as if in a trance)* I'm already asleep . . . the whole room is like smoke around me . . . and you look like a cast-iron stove . . . like a man dressed in black with a stovepipe hat . . . your eyes glowing like fading coals in a dying fire . . . your face like a patch of light. It's so nice and warm. And so bright . . . and so peaceful.

JEAN: *(putting the razor in her hand)* Here is the broom. Go now, while it's bright, out to the barn—and . . . *(he whispers in her ear)*

JULIE: *(coming to, a little)* Thank you. Now I'm going to my rest. But tell me one thing—that the first can also receive the gift of grace. Say it—even if you don't believe it!

JEAN: The first? I can't. But, wait. Miss Julie—I know what I can tell you! You're no longer one of the first—you're one of the last!

JULIE: That's true! I'm one of the last. I am the *very* last. Oh! . . . But now I can't go. Tell me just once more to go!

JEAN: Now I can't either! I can't!

JULIE: And the first shall be the last!

JEAN: Don't think, don't think! You're taking all my strength away, I'm getting weak. What? I thought the bell moved. . . . No! I should stuff some paper in it—afraid of a bell! But it isn't just a bell. There's somebody behind it. A hand sets it in motion. And something else sets the hand in motion. Cover your ears—cover your ears! But he'll just ring louder! He'll just keep ringing until someone answers.— And then it's too late! And then the police come— and then—

(The bell rings twice loudly. Jean flinches, then straightens up.)

It's horrible! But there's no other way!—Go!

(Miss Julie walks resolutely out through the door)